Date
Diary

Picture by the Tucker Sisters
2021

Date
Diary

Memoirs of Chrissy's Embarrassing Encounters

LISA SPRIGGS

THE CHOIR PRESS

First published in the United Kingdom in 2021 by
The Choir Press

ISBN 978-1-97863-233-0

Contents

Preface

*T*hrough life we meet some strange characters who we may not always understand or like, but maybe in a different time or place they could have been the one. I look back on my dating days and think that, if this didn't happen or this wasn't said, maybe things would have worked out differently.

This book is dedicated to everyone out there who has ever been on a really embarrassing date: nearly all of us. After years of experience on the dating scene and many of the same embarrassing moments, I realised I was becoming an expert on strange types of dates. Although at the time I would blame myself for them going wrong one way or another, I can safely say that things happen for a reason and they always turn out for the best, letting you find something better in life.

This book has been written purely in the hope that the reader will have a good chuckle to themselves.

All the characters and dates in this book are fictional, but they are also relatable (to a degree) and I'm sure they will give you as much enjoyment reading them as I have had writing about them.

Thank you to my hubby for sitting and listening to me in hysterics night after night as I wrote this book. Thank you to my little brother, who has given me constant sound advice and help throughout writing this book as he has experience on the dating scene. Also, a big thank you to my dear friend Shirley for reading the book for me and giving me her sound advice too. Thank you to my four beautiful daughters for giving Mummy some quiet time each day (throughout lockdown) to write this book.

Preface

My only hope for the future is that none of my daughters or yours will ever have to go on any dates similar to those in this book. However, once you have read it, I think we'll all agree it's very likely that they will.

Enjoy reading!

CHAPTER 1

How It All Began

L ying on the bed in floods of tears, feeling as though my life was now ruined. OK, so I know it sounds like I'm being melodramatic, but it seriously was ruined. I was nearly forty years old now, with no children, slightly overweight, and it would be an understatement to say I hadn't been feeling so great since I got chucked by my sleazeball boyfriend. At one point he'd declared his undying love for me, but now it seemed he couldn't stand the sight of me.

In the few days since his message, all I seemed to have done was gain a few more pounds and a drink problem. I never managed to sober up for very long before my broken heart was hurting so much that I'd pour myself another.

I couldn't believe that, after I'd dedicated a good part of my thirties to him, he had decided I was no longer his cup of tea. Really? No, not really; he'd dumped me for a gorgeous blonde twenty-something, Jessie with the big boobs and no brain. The only comfort I could take from this was that her boobs would eventually start to sag, and hopefully she would get the required half a brain cell to figure him out sooner than I did. Still, I'd had six years to do that and I hadn't managed it, so I wouldn't hold my breath.

I knew who Jessie was; I had briefly worked with her, but I must say she didn't last very long and was considered to be too big for her boots by a few of the people in the office. I would say too big for her bra, but hey-ho. I really don't want to sound jealous of them at all, but she had stolen him from me, and her ginormous boobs were the main thing I remembered about her. Every single male colleague of mine dropped his jaw at the sight of her, and some of the not-so-single ones too. Including my Ralph. In hindsight I had made the biggest mistake of my life inviting him to the office party that gave the two of them a chance meeting, and obviously now I was the one who was going to live with that for the rest of my lonely life.

I couldn't help but wonder how my life had all gone so wrong. I had a comfortable childhood with parents who never argued because Mum was always right. A lovely home life with no worries apart from homework that I never seemed to complete on time. I attended a very middle-class school on the outskirts of Nottinghamshire, where everyone was destined to do well.

I had always been popular at school, especially with the boys. Some of my old school friends had since amounted to nothing, and one lad I went out with, who was supposed to be an aspiring football player, had ended up still living with his parents and doing nothing with himself. I knew this because his mother had offloaded onto my mother and my mother had said, 'You've had a lucky escape there, Chrissy.' Although I'm not a snob, even I know any job is better than no job. I definitely had a lucky escape there, although his family were quite wealthy, so I guess I could have been a kept woman if I had ended up with the loser, living off his parents too.

I had a few not-so-serious boyfriends in my teens. They all seemed to have amounted to nothing too, but at the time they bragged about what they were going to achieve. Bullshit! My best friend from that time, Helen, however, had moved away and was a very successful reporter down south. I missed her dearly, but I certainly couldn't ring her to let her know I'd been dumped, as she had never liked Ralph and would just say, 'I told you he was a waste of space.'

In my twenties I had men falling over themselves for my

attention. I don't want to blow my own trumpet, but I knew from all the male attention I had always got that I was what you would call easy on the eye. The only thing was that I just wasn't looking for love. I was out to have fun and had many short encounters that amounted to nothing. Some lasted longer than others, but the bottom line was that I didn't really care too much about what happened or how it ended. My main and only concern was payday at the end of the month, which meant I could pay off all my debts (which my parents knew nothing about) and then get back into debt by wasting money on clothes and partying every weekend.

I never really was the settling-down type, so I wasted most of my time on very attractive men who made me look even better in their flash cars. A couple were much older than me, with money (obviously), and ended up almost being like a concerned dad. Let's just say that these relationships did not last long at all. I already had a dad and thought they were boring and controlling, telling me my skirt was too short or I wore too much makeup: seriously!

Most of my love encounters in my twenties were much younger, though, and not so serious. They would be more than happy to only see me occasionally for my crown jewels. Some I'd never hear from them again: surprise, surprise! Sometimes this made me feel really used, but most of the time I have to be honest and say I felt exactly the same way about them, as they were very selfish lovers. Having said that, though, when one did fall off the radar I would be completely gutted and tell all my friends he was the love of my life and I was never going to get over him. Then I'd be upset for a day or so, or at least until someone else caught my eye – or should I say before I caught their eye, which, believe me, wasn't usually very long at all.

Then, in my early thirties, I wasted most of my time being so picky that nobody seemed good enough. I wrote a list of pro's and con's about everything, hence my listmaking skills. However, sometimes my list became ridiculous, with things on there like *Must be able to drive and have a sports car* (I had become accustomed to this in my twenties). Another of my favourite pros was *Must have a super-fit body with tight cheeks.* I know, looking back, this does sound stupid, especially since I've not been able to keep my own little (or not-so-little) bum tight.

Anyway, some of my lists for potential boyfriends use to be really long, with over twenty-five qualities on there. After a few years I realised I was not going to find anyone who would live up to all these expectations, and I certainly wasn't going to find that in my thirties when all my ideal boyfriends were looking for someone at least ten years my junior, so eventually I thought I'd settle for a not-so-good-looking guy who was reliable and honest.

Well, that's what I thought I had when I met Ralph. He wasn't that bad-looking, but we were once referred to as Beauty and the Beast by one of my so-called friends. Although I wasn't happy about it at the time, on reflection there must have been some truth in what she had said about us. He did resemble Piers Morgan, so not the best-looking of the bunch. As far as I was concerned, though, I'd found someone I could trust and, more importantly, had fallen in love with: someone I was going to grow old with.

We had so many cosy holidays together at my mum and dad's holiday home (for free, of course): a luxury sea-view caravan in Cornwell. What more could he have asked for? If not for anything else, he could at least have stayed with me just for the free holidays once a year. Or what about our late-night chats? Weren't they important? (Or was it only me who'd miss them?)

Six years later I was left with no man, no children and no

integrity. I was now stalking him and his new girlfriend online. Didn't feel great, but that was all I had on my lonely evenings with a bottle of red as my new best friend.

Every time I saw pictures of the pair of them looking happy and snug on his or her social media profile, I literally felt sick. I had drunken visions of going round to his and doing something drastic like playing loud romantic music. 'Endless Love' or 'My Heart Will Go On' were the two favourites; those were our songs, so they'd be the obvious choice. I imagined singing them loudly up to his bedroom window. But then I'd also imagine she'd be in there and shout out to me to piss off. Then I'd shout something childish back, like 'He's only with you for your tits,' and walk off crying.

Sometimes I imagined turning up at his workplace, where I knew she wouldn't be, and asking him, 'Are you going to take me back yet, or are you staying with her?' But then I'd remember exactly what his new girlfriend looks like, and I'm definitely not a match for her. If there was a cross between Marilyn Monroe and Dolly Parton, then that's her. Don't get me wrong: if it was a pub quiz or a crossword, I'm sure I'd win hands down, but, let's be honest, no one's going to give up playing with her knockers all night for me. I just had to accept I had been defeated and I needed to move on.

Can you believe, after six years together, the loser even ended it by sending me a text?

Hi babe, sorry but I'm thinking things between us aren't working out and you really deserve someone much better than me. Hope you find what you want in life. Take care. X

First of all, what's the kiss for when he's dumping me, and secondly, what did he mean by 'find what you want'? Was it that I mentioned us having kids, or was it that I asked him to move in? **Tip for my future self:** *never ask either of those two things again.*

After all this I just couldn't help but feel low about it all. I'd given him some of the best years of my life.

I decided to pick myself up. I was going to down the contents of a bottle of red wine or two and make a list that would help me find Mr Right before my childbearing days were totally gone. I could do this!

1. *Good sense of humour*
2. *Tall (with big feet, of course)*
3. *Speaks Latin (Italian or Spanish will do)*
4. *Has loads of money (a good job will do)*
5. *Nice teeth*
6. *Nice home*
7. *Good-looking*
8. *Good listener*
9. *Good kisser*
10. *NO CHILDREN (well, not until they're with me, anyway)*
11. *Clean and smells good*
12. *Knows how to have a good time*
13. *My parents like him*

I was starting to wonder whether I was being too ambitious, so I backtracked and removed the last three from the list. Number 11, I figured I could always make him wash before any hanky-panky. Number 12, he might know how to have too much of a good time, and that's never good. Number 13, all in-laws hate each other; isn't that just normal?

So this was my final list:

1. *Good sense of humour*
2. *Tall (with big feet)*
3. *Speaks Latin (Italian or Spanish will do)*
4. *Has loads of money (a good job will do)*
5. *Nice teeth*
6. *Nice home*
7. *Good-looking*
8. *Good listener*
9. *Good kisser*
10. *NO CHILDREN (well, not until they're with me)*

Ten things I should be able to find in a man. Surely this couldn't be that difficult.

OK, so my next thought was 'how am I going to find him?' All the younger girls at work were raving on about online dating; how hard could that be? They had never directly talked to me about it, because they clearly thought I was too old and had to be married by now, but I had overheard them having many conversations about it.

Right, I know: I'll have a look at dating site reviews online, have a think about the ones that sound the best and then go for one.

Yes, that sounded like a plan. Then I could join and have a nosey around on there to get a feel for it. Hopefully I would only have to go on one date and find Mr Right.

I started by looking up the dating sites I knew of; I had overheard a few names, so I decided to Google them. I soon realised that, unless I was looking to drop my pants within the first five minutes, I was not going to last on any of these sites for long. I certainly wouldn't be meeting Mr Right; just Mr A Bit Of Right Fun. I was past all that now, and it really just wasn't my style.

I'd really hoped I was going to find love by meeting someone in the old-fashioned way: you know, exchanging numbers while flirting in a seedy bar. However, given that my best friend Jayne had settled down now and could never find a babysitter (although she could really leave them with their dad; I never say this, of course) and my other best friend Helen had moved down to London, I was kind of left with just Sally from work, who was in a relationship with a total loser who always put her down (again, I'd never say this out loud). My friendship choices were limited, and I really didn't want to hit the town alone. I just couldn't go hanging around bars looking desperate, especially at my age, so I had to rethink what I could do.

I know, I thought, *I'll buy a newspaper and go through the lonely hearts column, like people used to years ago.*

Because I was so desperate at that moment in time, I quickly got ready and went straight to my local newsagent's. Trying to be discreet, I had a little look through a well-known newspaper, I couldn't find the page. *Damn,* I thought, *I bet they've stopped doing all that now.* It was 2005 and the internet had completely taken over, what with online dating being so popular.

I picked up another newspaper and I couldn't find the page in there either. Oh no; this was a disaster.

I decided to go to the alcohol aisle and picked up an overpriced bottle of red. Although I was well stocked at home, at least I'd look as though I was in there for something, and you could never really have enough bottles of red.

As I was about to pay at the counter, I saw a pile of local newspapers. I picked one up, hoping they still had a lonely hearts page in there, and started flicking through. *Yes,* I thought, *there is a god;* I'd found one small section on a page towards the back of the paper. I smiled at the man serving and said, 'This too, please.' Then I got out of there as quickly as possible, just in case any of my neighbours had seen me acting very strangely with a bottle of wine and a newspaper.

Back at home, I started searching through the two small columns, all of which were completely desperate ads. I knew I had to try one, no matter how strange it seemed.

OK, so, working from what I had read, some of my list would not apply. Was I dropping my standards again? Clearly yes, but, if I wanted to find someone within the next few weeks, marriage in a year or two, and a baby in three, it had to be worth a go.

Then an ad caught my eye:

Tall, dark and handsome
45-year-old man
seeking 35 years plus lady
with a good sense of humour.

Bingo, I thought to myself. Surely this was a hidden message that he was into plus-size girls. He was the right age, and I'd be ticking at least number 2 (tall), number 7 (good-looking) and possibly number 3 (speaks Latin, or close enough) off my list, if the 'dark' meant Italian or Spanish. I could be on to a winner here.

Well, the fact that he was asking for a lady with a good sense of humour could also mean ticking number 1 off my list, and I certainly did have a good sense of humour. Maybe he'd have big feet too, which is always welcome, as we all know what they say about big feet.

I decided to respond to his advert, so I called his voicemail PO box number and left a very awkward drunken message. I left my name and a mention that I met his description of a desirable woman. Oh, yes, and my mobile number too, so he could text me if he was happy to.

Nothing happened overnight, but, sure enough, three days later I got a text that made my day. He seemed to really want to meet me too. Yes!

CHAPTER 2

Tall Man with Big Feet

It was the night of my first real date in a long time: five weeks, to be exact, since I'd been chucked. I was really excited.

All day I wondered about what I was going to wear. I didn't want to turn up looking like I was wearing a sign saying *ride me*, but I also didn't want to turn up looking like I definitely needed Vagisan (no offence to all those who do need Vagisan). This was a very difficult decision, so I chose to consult my dear friend Jayne, who had been married for many years, with wonderful children, and had been able to keep her man happy successfully whilst holding down a full-time job. In my books, this was a woman I should take advice from, friend or not.

I picked up the phone and dialled her number. Jayne answered, as always reliable and available to take my nuisance calls.

After a good twenty minutes she had talked me into wearing a sensibly lengthened dress. The only problem was that the one I had in mind was a size too small, but what the hell: the tighter, the better. When I was getting ready this was a bit of a problem, but I managed to squeeze into it anyway. The time was drawing closer to 8pm, so I had to really get my skates on.

An hour later, with hair and makeup done, I ordered my taxi. I downed two gin and tonics: one for courage and the other for good luck. Soon the taxi arrived, and I was on my way to meet my date.

As I walked into the bar that we had arranged to meet at, I could sense people looking at me. *Ooh,* I thought to myself, *I must be looking good in this dress.* Thinking nothing more of it, I scanned the bar area and laid my eyes on the most gorgeous-looking man. He slightly nodded, so I started making a beeline for him.

Just then I glanced at myself in a mirror to my right and saw two lumps of skin cream around my neck area that I had forgotten to rub in. It looked like someone had given me a pearl necklace. Thinking on my feet, I quickly looked around and saw a sign for the bathroom, so I nodded at the man at the bar and made a detour to the ladies'.

Shit, shit, I thought. *Now he's going to think I've been on a very successful date earlier, or he may think he's turned up to a very successful date. I've definitely not signed up for anything like that, so he can get that out of his head.* Either way, this was not a good start.

I rubbed in the cream and walked out to the bar area to face the music. As I walked to the bar, looking straight at the same gorgeous man, I heard someone behind me call my name: 'Chrissy?'

I quickly turned around and had to look up. This had to be him. 'Hi,' I said. 'Are you Tony?'

'Yes, that's me,' he replied.

Scanning him discreetly, I was very impressed. He was very tall and, looking down, I noticed he had enormous feet. *Interesting,* I thought. He was already ticking all the boxes I had previously ticked for him. I was over the moon that he hadn't witnessed my earlier mishap too.

We sat down to our table reservation, and I quickly picked up that we seemed to be very attracted to one another. We hardly looked anywhere other than at each other all night.

This was definitely Mr Right for me. He had lovely teeth and a full dark head of hair. He wasn't Mediterranean and didn't speak any other languages, but, given everything else, I was more than happy to cross that quality off my list. He reminded me of a tall version of Tom Cruise, if there's such a thing.

It was a lovely evening outside, with it being the middle of summer, so he said he would walk me home. Such a gentleman, I thought to myself. We strolled along, still chatting about anything and nothing, but all the time I was thinking how lucky I was. This time I had definitely landed on my feet.

As we approached mine, we made plans to see each other again. He gently kissed me on my cheek and said bye. I was smitten, truly and utterly.

The next day, all I could do was think about him. When my phone pinged, I hoped it was him. It wasn't, though; it was only my mum, asking why I hadn't arrived yet for Sunday dinner. I told her I'd be over soon.

I took a quick shower and slipped on jeans and a T-shirt, then made my way over there. Mum and Dad lived near me, so I regularly popped round for dinner. It was lovely to see them, and Mum was a great cook, but it also saved me a lot of money on shopping and a lot of time on cooking. It was the perfect setup, really, especially as I was still always living in my overdraft.

My mum asked me a couple of times, 'Why are you sitting there daydreaming?'

'Oh, it's nothing,' I'd reply. I really didn't want to mention anything just yet, as I knew my love life always worried them. They always seemed to think I'd get heartbroken again, as that seemed to be the story of my life so far. *Not this time,* I thought to myself.

*

Over the next three weeks, we exchanged naughty texts and went on three more mindblowing dates; no hanky-panky, of course. That was when he asked me the big question: 'Do you want me to stay over tonight?'

Well, I definitely did, so I just replied, 'Yes, of course,' without hesitation.

That evening was lovely. We sat watching an old DVD and chatting away to each other; our conversations seemed to just flow. I couldn't help but think this was how we were going to live the rest of our lives together.

One thing led to another and, before you know it, we were in the bedroom. It was the most amazing experience, to say the least, then we fell asleep in each other's arms. This feeling was truly bliss!

In the middle of the night, I had a lovely dream about me and Tony, where he was laughing and telling me how deeply he had fallen in love with me. Just then I started to wake up and realised he was at the foot of the bed, but still talking.

As I woke up properly, it dawned on me that this wasn't a dream. The man of my dreams, Mr Right, who I was supposed to spend the rest of my life with, was holding my feet and talking to them.

'I knew you were the one when I first laid eyes on you,' he said to my foot. 'Come here and give me a kiss.'

I could feel him putting his tongue between my toes. The only way I could describe it was that he was French kissing my left foot.

Dear God, how awkward. What do I do now? Do I pretend to stay asleep and then never mention it again? Or do I let him know I'm awake and ask him what the frigging heck he is doing to my poor feet?

I almost decided to let him carry on licking them for a bit, as it did feel nice and could be part of our foreplay, but then I thought, *No, this is just weird; he knows I'm asleep.* I pretended to move into a different sleeping position to get him away from them. He must have got the message or had enough fun by then, because he went back up to the head of the bed and cuddled me from behind.

Too distraught to know what to do, I lay there for the rest of the night, finding it very difficult to go back to sleep and also feeling very worried for my poor feet.

In the morning he was awake, seeming very happy with himself, and kissed me goodbye as he had to leave for work. I was left thinking to myself, *What am I going to do now?* The man of my dreams turned out to be a complete weirdo with a foot fetish. I definitely wasn't prepared to have my feet abused like that again – well, not without my consent – so there was only one thing for it.

I kindly let him know by text I wasn't going to see him any more, and gave him the cheap excuse that I wasn't looking for anything serious. How ironic; I'd turned into my nasty ex. The truth was that I was desperately looking for something serious with someone exactly like him, minus the fetish. I'd made the right choice, though, as I really didn't want to live the rest of my life worried for my poor feet every night. Number 2 was definitely getting crossed off my list.

1. *Good sense of humour*
2. ~~*Tall (with big feet)*~~
3. *Speaks Latin (Italian or Spanish will do)*
4. *Has loads of money (a good job will do)*
5. *Nice teeth*
6. *Nice home*
7. *Good-looking*
8. *Good listener*
9. *Good kisser*
10. *NO CHILDREN (well, not until they're with me)*

CHAPTER 3
Spanish Stallion

A couple of weeks had gone by and I was still feeling totally gutted. After three weeks of dating a totally amazing man, he becomes the foot monster. I was sure that this could only happen to me. I was really pleased I'd never mentioned him to Mum, at least, or I would never have heard the last of it. I was still totally gutted about Ralph, and if he wanted me I would take him back in a heartbeat.

OK, so I had two choices: either I give up and face the fact that I am going to grow old all alone with nobody to love me, or I get straight back out there on another date. Neither thought was very appealing, but I chose the latter. If nothing else, I am at least a tryer.

I knew I had to do a bit of food shopping, so I quickly got dressed and went straight out with one thing on my mind: another newspaper. Now that I'd crossed *tall (with big feet)* off my list, I'd hopefully find something different.

When I got back home, I put everything away and sat down with another local newspaper; I'd checked in the more popular tabloids, but I still couldn't find any lonely hearts pages. The industry must really have been sizzling out, what with the internet blowing up, but, luckily for me, the local ones were still printing the page.

I went straight to the section for lonely hearts and started reading through the columns. Suddenly one caught my eye.

Very good-looking
Spanish stallion looking
for an English queen.

Ooh, this really does sounds promising, I thought, so as before I responded to the ad. I left pretty much the same message as I had for the foot monster, obviously hoping this one would be nothing like that.

I waited patiently for days, but then I got the reply I wanted. Well, sort of; it was in broken English, but with my savvy detective skills I could just about work out his messages. He had asked to meet me that weekend, and I was quite surprised by some of the places he suggested; they really weren't the sort of place I'd usually go, so I kept texting back, *Anywhere else?* This seemed to prompt him into making other suggestions, and eventually he suggested a bar that I had heard had a lot of interesting stage acts. If nothing else, I thought this could be fun, but how very strange. I just had to give it a try, as maybe he could be the one.

A few days later and it was the evening of my date with my Spanish stallion. I pictured us having lovely little babies with curly dark hair. I also pictured us taking lovely holidays in sunny Spain. I needed to make sure I didn't ruin my chances, so that evening I made a real effort: nothing too revealing, but certainly something to catch his eye, showing a little bit of cleavage. I must admit, I was very excited to be meeting a Spaniard, and it certainly couldn't go worse than the last man I had met.

As I was about to leave I thought maybe the place would be busy, so I texted him to say I'd be wearing a red scarf. Surprisingly, he replied, *Me too.* Oh, OK; that was good, then. Well, sort of odd, but at least we would be able to identify each other.

As soon as I walked through the door, he was up off his seat clapping. He seemed awfully overenthusiastic, but it was nice to be entering the bar with such a welcome. I almost felt famous.

My heart was racing as he waved me over to the table, I was pleasantly surprised by how gorgeous this man was; wow. I'd heard of the Italian stallion, but he topped what my ideal man would look like. He had very nice teeth, good hair, and he was Spanish. Four ticks off my list straight away.

On the flipside, I did wonder why he was dressed so revealingly. Calling him flamboyant would have been an understatement. He was wearing an open bright red shirt, very tight shiny black leggings and a red silk scarf. How strange, I thought. Maybe it was just a Spanish thing.

He kept shouting, 'Bonita, Bonita,' which I also thought was very strange. To be completely honest, my real thoughts were that this was not flipping normal at all, but again I naively said to myself, *It must just be a Spanish thing.* I know that I am alright-looking, and some would say easy on the eye, but even I knew that he shouldn't be this flipping excited to see me. Maybe it was the language barrier, as there were no other words spoken between us. He gave me quite a few big smiles and the odd tap on the back, but other than that I just sat there nursing my drink.

Then, as the lights started to dim, I realised that the show was about to begin. My date was up out of his seat again, and at that point I knew what all this excitement was about. My date was clearly waiting for the drag act to start.

Then came the announcement that drag queen Bella Bonita would soon be taking the stage.

Half shocked and half curious, I wondered, *Is he gay? Is this the English queen he's looking for?* Thinking about it, I'd never said whether I was a woman or a man, but I hadn't thought I needed to.

My mind was racing now. *Oh, dear God, does he think I'm a man in drag?* This was turning out very awkward indeed. I was open to a lot of things in my desperate search, but I was

17

certainly not going to pretend I was in drag just to get a boyfriend, and eventually he'd find out anyway when I couldn't produce the goods.

Just then Bella Bonita came on stage, strutting her stuff, dressed in sequins and feathers. She started to sing the classic 'It's Raining Men', which seemed to be going down very well with everyone, including my date, and, although the little shit hadn't said two words to me in the two hours I'd been sitting here, he was now singing fluently in English along to the song. Then all of a sudden he was on his feet again, but this time he went over to the front of the stage, literally screaming her name: 'Bella Bonita!'

OK, this is totally weird, I thought.

After drinking quite a few sexes on the beach, I then decided I had two choices: either I could walk out of this place and go home to a lonely empty flat, or I could join in with the fun, even if my date wanted Bella Bonita more than he wanted me. I chose to stay, get more drunk and have a bloody good night.

So there we were, the pair of us, clapping and singing along. I must admit it was the most fun I had had in weeks, and just for a moment I forgot all about my sad little life with no man. We must have looked like the two happiest people in this very busy bar, but, as all good things come to an end, so did this: a really good night of music and plenty of cocktails, but he definitely was not Mr Right, and neither was I. Mr Right, for him, was a man who was also wearing some extremely tight leggings and a tight, feathery pink top; this became apparent as my date had his tongue in this man's mouth for part of the evening. He definitely didn't want me and I definitely didn't want him, but overall it was a very good night out. I had certainly made a friend for life, or so I told myself whilst totally intoxicated.

Back home I dropped into bed – alone, of course – and thought, *This is not going to put me off trying to find love.* Now I was even more determined to find someone. However, number 3 was getting crossed off my list, as I had slightly been put off Latin-speaking men after this experience.

1. *Good sense of humour*
2. ~~*Tall (with big feet)*~~
3. ~~*Speaks Latin (Italian or Spanish will do)*~~
4. *Has loads of money (a good job will do)*
5. *Nice teeth*
6. *Nice home*
7. *Good-looking*
8. *Good listener*
9. *Good kisser*
10. *NO CHILDREN (well, not until they're with me)*

CHAPTER 4

Online Mr Scary

After my last two dates, I'd realised that I needed to try something different; clearly the lonely hearts weren't all that. So I decided to give this online dating stuff a try after all. I mean, how much worse could it be? I figured that at least I could see a photo of the person first; well, so I'd heard whilst eavesdropping in the office.

I chose one of the most well-known sites (again, only what I'd overheard) and signed up. Apparently, I could swipe left for no or right for yes depending on the look of someone or whether we had the same interests.

Looking through tonnes and tonnes of pictures. I seemed to be swiping left to all of them. Most were definitely too young for me, but, alarmingly, even more of them looked very desperate.

Then I thought, *Oh, what the hell, I've got nothing to lose; I just have to give this a go.*

I chose a man who looked a bit older than the rest of them, but I must admit he wasn't my usual type. The fact he'd said on his profile that he was really keen to meet a mature woman seemed to fit the bill. He'd also put that he had a really nice place, so I was imagining a swanky flat on the riverbank.

I pondered for a while and then said to myself, *Just go for it, Chrissy.* So I swiped right and waited to see if we were matched.

Sure enough, he obviously swiped right for me too, because a few days later I was able to send him a private message. I sent one: *Hi, I'm Chrissy.*

And he replied almost instantly saying, *Hi, how are you, I have a nice place, I would like to meet you.*

I must admit this did sound strange to me, but also promising, to be fair, so I decided to give it a go.

We exchanged numbers and chatted on the phone several times. He mentioned his ex-girlfriend quite a bit, who had dumped him for his so-called friend. I mentioned I'd been through the same experience recently too; it seemed we had a connection.

A couple of weeks had gone by and I asked him where he would like us to meet. He replied that anywhere would suit him so long as it was near the city. This was a broad answer, but the city was good for me too, as it meant I could get a bus home easily at the end of the night.

Anyway, he suggested a pub on the outskirts of the city, I had never heard of it, but I did know that that side of town wasn't that nice. *What the hell,* I thought. (This seemed to be becoming my motto lately.) *He could be worth a chance.*

A week went by, and finally it was the day of potentially meeting my Mr Right. As I did most Saturdays, I decided to do my morning food shopping at Sainsbury's; this was to make sure I was stocked up on red wine for my Saturday evening with the laptop, still stalking my ex. Although this Saturday I'd be out on my date, I still thought I'd better stock up for the week ahead.

While I was there, I got caught in the middle of a traumatic event. A man in a big sheepskin coat was running in my direction, holding something that looked rather like a jar of coffee, with the security guard in hot pursuit. The thief knocked me out of the way, but then, because I fell into a magazine stand, I got in the way of the security guard who was trying to catch him; as a result of all this, the man got away. I felt terribly sorry and did apologise profusely; the security guard seemed more interested in making sure I was OK. I assured him I was and left the shop.

Instead of going home I went to my parents' house to have a cup of tea, as I really was quite shaken up. As soon as I thought of tonight's date, though, I felt better. Remembering I had a date with the online gentleman, potentially Mr Right, was just the remedy I needed.

I gave my parents both a kiss and told them I felt much better after offloading my ordeal onto them (in a nice way, of course). They knew me and understood.

That evening I choose to dress quite casually as it was a date in a pub. I didn't know what to expect as I didn't know the place, so I put on casual jeans with a nice blouse and, of course, a pair of heels. Being only five foot nothing, I always needed a height boost.

I received a text saying he was on his way to the pub now. *I'd better get my skates on, then,* I thought.

As I walked into the pub, I realised it was even rougher than I had imagined. Firstly, it had a very fusty smell. Secondly, the only other person in there was a woman sitting at the bar, covered in tattoos, with her head shaven. I couldn't help but feel slightly scared. Very quietly I ordered a gin and tonic and took it to sit at a small table in the corner of the room.

Soon after I had sat down, a man walked in. I was sure I'd seen him before, but where? I'd never been in here before, and I didn't really go anywhere other than work and Sainsbury's on a Saturday morning. He was quite short, with a shaven head, and wearing a big sheepskin coat, just like the man I had seen that morning in Sainsbury's; it was exactly the same as Del Boy's in *Only Fools and Horses*. Then it dawned on me: *Shit, oh shit, it's him. Please, dear God, don't let it be him.*

He didn't say anything to me, just walked past me and went to the bar to order himself a drink. *Phew!* I thought. *Thank*

God. I just hoped he didn't recognise me, but why would he when he'd been more focused on his getaway with his coffee for free?

The man pulled out his phone and fiddled with it for a moment. Just then my phone went *ping*; I had received a message. I nearly didn't take my phone out of my handbag, but it was obvious where the ping had come from. The message read, **I'm waiting. x**

He must have heard the ping too, because he started to walk towards me. 'So you're Chrissy,' he said.

For a moment I nearly lied, but I knew I couldn't as he had already figured it out. I said, 'Yes,' in a timid voice. 'Yes, I am, and you must be Will.'

He sat down opposite me and finished his drink very quickly, then said, 'Come on, then; I've got a place we can go and have a coffee.'

Shocked at how forward he was being and thinking I really wasn't sure I wanted to drink his stolen coffee, I didn't know how to reply. To give myself a minute or two to ponder exactly what his invitation meant, I said, 'Shall we have another drink on me?'

He seemed quite happy with this, so I went to the bar and ordered another drink for us both. While I was ordering the drinks the very scary-looking lady sitting at the bar uttered under her breath, 'Watch yourself, love.'

I couldn't figure out if she was threatening me or trying to warn me. I thought about this as the barman poured our drinks. If she was threatening me, she would surely have approached me in an aggressive manner by now. Instead, she must have been talking about my date, so I nodded politely to let her know I understood. Now I started to think of excuses to get out of there safely.

For the next twenty minutes or so I didn't say a word, still in shock, while he talked about nothing but Tara, his ex who had left him for his friend. Although I was feeling quite physically threatened, emotionally I did have an understanding of his feelings of rejection. I certainly had mixed emotions, what with knowing I'd seen him shoplifting earlier (I didn't tell him this) and the fact that the lady at the bar had discreetly warned me about him. This was not turning out to be a very good date, or place, for that matter.

I offered to buy us another drink to buy myself more time. This time he told me to give him the money so he could go to get them. I did as he said, of course, and handed him a £10 note. He returned with the drinks, but he'd put the change in his pocket. I didn't dare to ask for it back.

At this point he seemed even more eager to leave and completely necked his drink.

That's when I said, 'I'm very sorry, but I'm not sure it's the right time of the month for me to go anywhere to do anything, if you get what I mean.' With this I gave him a little wink, thinking I was keeping the tone light.

To my surprise he just said, 'I'm ready when you are for that coffee,' as though he'd never heard me.

I repeated myself like I was a character in a pantomime: 'I'm very sorry, but I'm not sure it's the right time of the month for me to go anywhere to do anything, if you get what I mean,' giving another little wink.

'I don't care,' he replied. I couldn't work out if he thought he was being reassuring.

Then I kindly said, 'Well, I've really enjoyed meeting you, so would you like to rearrange to meet again without the distraction of having the painters in?'

He seemed to digest this information, gave a little laugh at my joke and agreed to meet the following week, same place, same time. Then he continued to pour his heart out about his ex for a bit longer, until I said, 'OK, well, I'd better get the half-past bus.'

He offered to walk me to the bus stop. I couldn't really say no and figured we were still in town (well, sort of), so I accepted his offer and we made our way out of the place. The tattooed lady at the bar looked at me in disgust and then looked away. Maybe she thought I was doing some sort of business with him.

Anyway, as we got near my bus stop, he asked me, 'Can you do me a really big favour?'

'Of course,' I replied, feeling my stomach turn.

He looked at me very seriously and asked, 'Can you lend me a fiver until the next time we meet?'

This was when I started to feel very sorry for him. Without hesitation I politely took the change from my pocket and gave it to him. He waited until he'd seen me get on my bus, then waved me off.

I sat there on the bus with very mixed emotions about him. I was relieved I was safely on my way home. But I felt very sorry for him, as I could see he was a broken man dumped by his no-good partner, just as I had been, and clearly needed some financial help. We weren't that different after all.

Having said this, I wouldn't ever be contacting him again and certainly didn't need the fiver back that much either. I also thought, *No more online dating for me.*

Back at home, I was safe and totally sober for once. I decided to cross number 6 off my list, as it didn't seem that important any more.

1. *Good sense of humour*
2. ~~*Tall (with big feet)*~~
3. ~~*Speaks Latin (Italian or Spanish will do)*~~
4. *Has loads of money (a good job will do)*

Date Diary

5. Nice teeth
6. ~~Nice home~~
7. Good-looking
8. Good listener
9. Good kisser
10. NO CHILDREN (well, not until they're with
    me)

CHAPTER 5
Toy Boy Mr Vain

Feeling totally deflated and fed up with dating, I threw myself into drinking more wine and more stalking; this was all I seemed to have now outside work.

I thought about ways to cheer myself up and decide to have a beauty treatment day at a posh spa. Jayne had told me about a really nice place that she used to love to go to; however, now that she had children, she never got the chance. I gave her a call and said I'd pay for her to come with me if she could get her other half, Mr So Reliable, to have the kids one Sunday.

Later that day she called me back, really happy and excited that he had agreed and she would finally get a break. This was just what I needed for myself, so, selfishly, I couldn't care less if she was getting a day away from the kids.

As soon as I came off the phone to her, I rang the number she had just given me and booked us in for that weekend. I booked in two treatments each and nearly passed out as they told me how much it had come to. I'd just have to put it on my credit card because, as usual, I didn't have any money.

Sunday morning, Jayne came to pick me up in her very practical seven-seater. I jumped in with my nicely packed little weekend bag. I noticed there were plenty of empty wrappers and crumbs and just looked at Jayne with a fake smile; she gave me the shoulder shrug and said she hadn't had time to clean out the car. This wasn't a big deal, but I hoped nothing would get stuck to my semi-new suede jacket.

As we hit the road, I started offloading onto Jayne about all the cosy pictures I kept seeing; it was really getting to me. She advised me once again to stop torturing myself by looking. I told her that I was going to try my best to stop and that today was about us. Well, me, really, but I said *us* as she was clearly over the moon to be coming with me.

On arrival we were shown around by a very good-looking and muscular young man, who seemed to be very over-friendly with me. Jayne gave me a wink a couple of times as she'd noticed this too. He was actually really funny and had us both in stitches with some of his witty comments. I did wonder how old he was; he was definitely a man, but clearly fifteen years or so my junior. But twenty-five years old is still an adult, of course, so I did a little flirting back with my eyes.

After he left us, we went into the ladies' changing rooms and got changed. Jayne jokingly fluttered her eyelids at me.

The beautiful heated open rooftop pool was amazing and, although I'm not a strong swimmer, I jumped at the chance to do some widths at the shallow end. I got a few funny looks, but I'd rather that than being out of my depth.

I was clearly totally out of shape and breathing heavily enough to make a lady give me a concerned look and then ask if I was alright. *Bloody cheek,* I thought, but I nodded politely. Of course I was flipping alright; I'd done nothing but consume large amounts of alcohol daily for the past few months, which had clearly taken its toll, but I was still quite perky in myself. Anyway, I'd be having lunch soon, and I'd make sure I drank plenty of whatever was on the menu then too.

I jumped out the pool and headed for the showers before using the steam room. Jayne had said she'd be swimming a bit longer, and I guess having to take her kids swimming every week had helped in one way.

As I sat quietly in the steam, thinking I was the only one in there, I let out a little trump. Just then the steam cleared slightly, and I could see there was a man sitting in the corner very quietly.

Damn, I thought. I wondered if he'd heard me. Or maybe he thought it was my bum cheeks slapping against the wet seating. More embarrassment; nothing seemed to go well for me. I decided not to say anything and sat as still as possible, just in case I made another noise that made me look more stupid than I already felt.

After what seemed like eternity the man stood up and made his way towards me. That's when I realised it was the young man who had shown us around earlier. Oh, this was even more embarrassing.

After he'd sat down near me, we ended up making small talk. His name was Sean, apparently. I realised he actually was coming on to me, and it became especially clear when he asked me to go on a date with him.

Although, after Mr Scary, I had promised myself I would stop going on strange dates, I thought it wouldn't be that bad, so I politely accepted. After all, I had met Sean face to face already and knew he had a job (and a very good bod and bum). I wondered where we would go, and just as I thought it the words came out of my mouth; I couldn't help but blurt it out.

He suggested going to an ice-skating rink. I'd never been on this sort of date before and part of me thought he was joking, but then I realised he was being serious. I burst out laughing and said, 'Yes, why not?'

We agreed to exchange numbers later. Although I probably could pass as his mother, I really did need a pick-me-up after all I'd been through lately.

Jayne found me in the Jacuzzi looking very smug and, when I told her what had happened, she laughed and laughed. 'Is that why you're in the Jacuzzi? Because you have the trumps?'

Very funny, Jayne. I told her she had spent too much time around children. 'Seriously, though, how old do you think he is?' I asked.

'No more than twenty-five,' she replied. We both laughed this time.

I told her he wanted to meet me at an ice rink, which I found funny.

'At least it's somewhere you can get to know each other without getting pissed,' she said. 'But don't be too surprised if you get mistaken for his mother.'

Shit, I thought to myself, *he really is young.* Oh, well; I had to give it a go. He was certainly ticking number 7, as he was absolutely handsome.

Soon it was time for our treatments: a facial and full body massage. This was a total delight, and at one point I think I half nodded off. I certainly made sure I didn't drop off too much because I couldn't bear trumping again. Jayne seemed to really enjoy her treatments too, and for a while we completely forgot all our troubles and relaxed in the moment. I bet she was super glad she had none of her children around ruining it for her, with their Mum this and Mum that.

After our treatments we went for lunch and, to my disappointment, the only drinks on the menu were completely alcohol-free. Jayne ordered a smoothie that turned up green and leafy. *She can't seriously drink that,* I thought, but she did. I just ordered a strong coffee. At least there was some incentive to drinking my drink: caffeine. We sat and chatted and laughed and chatted some more; this really was like old times.

The time passed us by so quickly, and we were soon on our way back to reality. Although I was totally gutted inside to be going back to my lonely little flat, I knew all good things came to an end eventually. Jayne dropped me off and we agreed to do it again some time; in my mind I was thinking, *Not on my bloody credit card again,* as it was going to take me a lifetime to pay off. When I walked through my front door, I couldn't help but go straight for the bottle of wine I'd left in the fridge to chill.

For once I went to sleep without overly stalking my ex or being totally blotto, I woke the next morning for work feeling really refreshed. I even looked better for having had such a relaxing and drink-free (well, almost free) weekend. I also felt quite positive about the date I had planned for the following weekend.

Throughout the week I surprisingly continued to feel a little better but still took to my usual evenings of wine and stalking.

*

Saturday morning, I got up and did my usual routine, although now I did my shopping at Asda instead of Sainsbury's just so I didn't take the chance of banging into Mr Scary. I stocked up on my usual weekly bottles of red and thought as a treat I'd get a litre bottle of pink gin and a litre bottle of vodka too. I was excited about my date and he might end up coming back to mine, so it'd be best to stock up even more than usual. I didn't know his age, which I was still very curious about.

A bit later that day I started to get ready. I decided to wear my only plain black tracksuit and a cute pair of Puma plimsolls that I'd had for many years but hardly wore, as this wasn't my everyday attire.

I'd arranged to meet Sean at the front entrance to the ice rink at 5pm. I felt very nervous and hoped we had things in common. I was totally desperate to find someone to spend my life with, and I just had to give this date a try in case he was Mr Right. There was also the fact that he could eventually save me a lot of money by being my live-in carer one day; this had its appeal too.

I decided to catch the bus up there and then walk the rest of the way, as I needed as much exercise as I could get if I was going to keep up with this spring chicken.

As I approached the main entrance, I could see Sean waiting for me, looking even younger than I remembered from the other day at the spa. I was going to turn around quickly, but he spotted me and called out my name. *Damn,* I thought, but I gave a very fake smile and waved at him.

He seemed overly eager to get in there, but, as we stood at the desk to pay, he just looked at me and didn't show any sign of getting his wallet out. When the girl told us the price he just smiled. To save myself from even more embarrassment, I just paid it for both of us.

I noticed he kept giggling, and I wondered whether he'd taken something as his eyes seemed red and glazed. Whatever he was on, he was acting very strangely.

We had to exchange our shoes for skates and then were shown through to a locker room where the attendant asked me if I would be sharing a locker with my son. Feeling even more embarrassed, I just nodded and smiled. I was cringing inside and knew I had to make some sort of excuse to get out of there.

When I turned to Sean, he had already started putting on his skates and seemed very eager to get on the ice. I, on the other hand, knew I couldn't skate and planned to take my time, so I could spend as little time on the ice as possible.

Eventually I got my skates on and looked up to see Sean already on the rink. To my surprise he was skating backwards on the ice, weaving in and out of people. Shit, was he some sort of pro? *No wonder he was keen to get in here,* I thought. *I'm really going to embarrass myself now.*

I got up and stumbled to the opening to the rink. Holding on to the side, I slowly started to walk around the edge, trying to find my balance.

As I held on to the side for dear life that prat just kept skating by, shouting stupid things like 'Show us what you've got, Chrissy!' and 'Chrissy, let go of the side!' Couldn't the plonker see I couldn't skate? He didn't even have the decency to come and help me, or at least slow down, acting like flipping Christopher Dean just to embarrass me even more.

I also noticed he was showing off to a group of girls who were no more than half my age and who clearly knew him. They kept looking over at me, which honestly made me feel like even more of an idiot. I'd paid for us to get in here just to risk my life, or at least risk breaking something.

Eventually, after what seemed like forever but really must have only been ten minutes or so, he must have realised I wasn't going to let go of the side and definitely wasn't going to attempt to skate on my own, so he came over and said, 'Do you want me to help you?'

I said, 'Yes, please, but can we go slowly? I've never done this before.'

Even as a child I was never that active or sporty. Colouring books and crayons would do me. My mother and father were forever trying to get me to do some sort of sport, but I just wasn't interested at all.

As I let go of the side and held on to him, I could feel how strong he was and noticed that he had beautiful skin too. I just couldn't help myself and asked, 'How old are you, Sean?'

I regretted it immediately as Sean looked at me and, with a giggle, he said, 'I'm nineteen.'

What? What? All sorts of things started racing through my mind. Was he pranking me? He did seem to be very jokey and childish. Was this really true? Oh, dear God, Chrissy, what the hell are you doing?

I wanted to run away, but all I could do was cling on to him, which must have given him the impression I was really keen on him; he was holding on to me very tightly too. I was desperate, but certainly not that desperate, by any stretch of the imagination. I politely said, 'Can you help me to get off the ice, please? I need the toilet.'

He helped me to the side, and then I stumbled to the seating area and couldn't get my skates off quick enough. The sooner I got the hell out of there, the better.

As he had followed me, I told him a rubbish lie about needing to get back home early to get some paperwork finished.

'Can we go and get a pizza first?' he asked.

He was acting like a ten-year-old at a bloody kids' party: first ice skating and now pizza. This was taking the biscuit, so at this point I snapped, what with everything I'd just been put through on the ice. 'No, we bloody well can't.'

And with that I stormed out of there and got home as quickly as I could to pour myself a large gin and tonic. I had hoped I'd be sharing it with him, but no chance of that, as he was barely even old enough to drink.

Oh, shit. Thinking about it, I really did sound like his mother, snapping like that.

This was another date ruined, and that made me even more sad and obsessive about Ralph. I didn't care how good-looking Sean was; number 7 was coming straight off my list.

All over before 7pm, and I was gutted. I just had to pull myself together, but not tonight. Tonight, I was getting sloshed and ringing poor Jayne to offload as usual. I vowed no more dating, as I was making terrible judgements through my desperation-tinted glasses.

1. *Good sense of humour*
2. ~~*Tall (with big feet)*~~
3. ~~*Speaks Latin (Italian or Spanish will do)*~~
4. *Has loads of money (a good job will do)*
5. *Nice teeth*
6. ~~*Nice home*~~
7. ~~*Good-looking*~~

8. *Good listener*
9. *Good kisser*
10. *NO CHILDREN (well, not until they're with me)*

CHAPTER 6
Work Colleague

*R*ight; with dating completely out of my mind for a bit, I had edited my list, which was now getting a lot shorter. I figured maybe things such as love would find me when it was time. This didn't make me any less desperate, but, after my last date, I had been brought back down to Earth. There were other things to focus on, so I concentrated on work and myself.

I signed up for an online self-awareness course with a view to getting an understanding of why I was feeling so unloved. I just stayed behind in the office for an extra hour or so a couple of times a week to complete it. The lady running the course seemed so grounded and self-assured, and I really wished I could be like that too.

We were asked to complete different assignments. One assignment about my childhood brought it to my attention that, although my mother and father loved me dearly and I had a great childhood, I had missed out on a lot of time with them. When I was writing things down on paper it became apparent that my parents were never around much; was this what my needy personality was about? Both my parents worked long hours and were very successful at what they did; most people would say they set a good example for me, with their strong work ethics. Being an only child, I was terribly spoilt and very rarely heard the word *no*. This self-awareness course was certainly helping me learn how to take responsibility for my own life and happiness and to stop blaming others.

For a while I was feeling better most days whilst out at work and busy, but by the evening I'd be alone again and feeling sorry for myself, so most evenings I'd open another bottle with the intention of only drinking one glass. It was never just one, though, and then I'd start to stalk you-know-who and his young, beautiful girlfriend with her two big friends.

Throughout the week I woke up feeling rough most days, but after a coffee or two I'd perk up and get into work, where I found solace in being busy and having some company. I tried to carry on as normal, and to the outside world I must have been doing a good job of putting on a brave face.

This was when I noticed a guy from work was clearly flirting with me on a day-to-day basis. He was leaving notes on my desk saying silly things like *Pay us more* and *Overworked & underappreciated.* I must admit they made me smile on occasion and were also very true, to say the least. Anyway, though, all I knew about this guy was that he had a terrible reputation in the office and had slept with a couple of my colleagues: only one-night stands, though.

For some reason I still decided to take him up on his offer of a few drinks one night after work. Desperate times call for desperate measures, I said to myself, even if it did mean having my colleagues' leftovers. I'd overheard he was a fantastic kisser: number 9, ticked.

With this in mind, I did what all us women do in this situation and started to tell myself that he liked me much more than any of the others. Obviously with me he would behave differently, like a true gentleman.

Towards the end of the week, I was clearly flirting with him too and also trying to indirectly find out any more information on him. For some reason, though, everyone stayed schtum. I figured he couldn't be that bad, or most of the girls would be calling him at the first opportunity.

We agreed to just go for some casual drinks after work; to me this was still a date. We left the office together and walked into an area nearby that was full of wine bars. Throughout the night we flirted some more and had a bloody good laugh, mainly at our colleagues' expense.

Then he asked, 'Do you want to come back to mine?'

I really needed to be sensible here; I didn't want to do anything that would embarrass me back in the office on Monday morning. I thought about it for a few seconds and decided, *Oh, what the hell. You only live once.* (My famous motto was back.) So we left the bar, and off we went to hail a cab.

Half an hour or so later, I was sitting in a very peculiar room full of pictures and posters of naked women. I mean, I had heard things about him that made him sound like a sex addict, but this was taking the piss. I felt like I was sitting in some sort of motionless orgy.

He poured us each a very strong gin and tonic and started to make small talk as though these photos weren't there. That's when I realised that I should just relax and go with the flow. He actually did seem quite funny, so at least number 1 on my list had been ticked, and to each their own and all that. Who was I to judge when I had a poster of Simon Cowell in my spare room?

The night continued to flow perfectly well, and after a few more drinks he got up and said, 'Right, I'm going to change into something a little more comfortable.'

I just sat there and gave a nod of acknowledgement. My mind was curious as to what he meant by *comfortable*. Joggers? PJs?

I waited for a while, and at one point wondered if he'd gone out as he was so quiet. That's when he walked in wearing a short, lacy red dress and a blonde bobbed wig.

My jaw must have hit the floor with total disbelief. I wanted to burst out laughing, but he looked at me so seriously that I managed to hold it in.

He introduced himself as Suzie. To my surprise I answered back, 'Hi, Suzie,' as though I was meeting this person for the first time.

Flipping hell, now what? I thought. *How am I going to deal with this?*

Suzie sat down beside me and continued chatting to me as before, but in a slightly higher-pitched voice. It was as though nothing had happened – well, for my colleague, anyway – but I was totally freaked out.

I asked to use the bathroom, so Suzie told me where it was. I really needed to get away; I couldn't hold in this laughter for much longer.

I also needed to think about how I was going to get out of this one. I have many friends from the LGBT community, but never had I been put in this sort of predicament. I'd gone home with Ian, a good-looking man from work who, by all accounts, had a healthy appetite for woman and a great sense of humour. Now I found myself sitting with Suzie with the blonde hair in a tiny flipping red dress. I didn't know whether my colleague was just a crossdresser or there was something more going on, but either way it was more than I was ready to handle on a first date. Think, Chrissy, think.

I know, I thought: *I'll say that my flatmate has texted me saying she has forgotten her key and is there any chance I can go back to let her in.* Yes, I lived alone, but he didn't know that. So I tried to compose myself and headed back downstairs to carry out my plan.

To my surprise, when I walked into the sitting room, he was gone. 'Ian?' I called out.

I listened carefully for a reply. I almost hoped he had gone out this time.

That's when a reply came from another room in his house. 'I'm in here,' he called out, in Suzie's high-pitched voice.

I really didn't want to go in there or to stay any longer. I panicked, shouted back, 'I'm sorry, Ian, but I've got to go,' and made a run for the door.

Feeling very confused by it all, I started to make my way home. It was a very long walk back to mine and it was pissing down with rain, but I'd take that over Suzie.

Another completely messed-up night, and I knew Monday morning I wasn't going to be able to look him in the face.

1. *Good sense of humour*
2. ~~*Tall (with big feet)*~~
3. ~~*Speaks Latin (Italian or Spanish will do)*~~
4. *Has loads of money (a good job will do)*
5. *Nice teeth*
6. ~~*Nice home*~~
7. ~~*Good-looking*~~
8. *Good listener*
9. ~~*Good kisser*~~
10. *NO CHILDREN (well, not until they're with me)*

CHAPTER 7
Nice Teeth Guy

Early one morning on the train to work, I began daydreaming about what my life would be like once I meet Mr Right. Cosy evenings together, relaxing holidays (well, until the kids came along).

Finally I snapped out of it and became aware that several people on the train were watching me, one of whom was a really nice-looking guy who kept glancing over at me and then back at the doors next to which he was standing. He seemed really shy, bless him.

I started to scan him up and down and noticed his clothes were rather dapper; he was also drop-dead gorgeous and had really nice teeth. I felt flattered and shyly gave him a little smile, so he knew I had noticed him and liked what I saw. I was hoping he was on this commute to work just as regularly as me, so we could keep flirting with our eyes and perhaps eventually talk to one another. I'd never seen him before, though.

As we approached a stop, he walked towards me and smiled. I felt very giddy, as he was even more gorgeous up close.

'Hi,' I said in a very quiet, shy voice.

That's when he slipped a card into my hand. 'Call me,' he said, and with that he walked back to the doors and waited for them to open.

I couldn't take my eyes off him, but as soon as he was out of sight I looked down at the card in my hand. Thinking out loud, I said, 'Wow, he's an architect.'

Everyone near me on the train looked at me, and I felt really stupid.

I started to picture our shared home: an enormous house with gorgeous Italian ceilings and chandeliers in the hallways. Yes, yes, I'd definitely landed on my feet here. That I didn't shout aloud, though.

That night, after a couple of glasses of my usual, I felt a bit of Dutch courage and I couldn't help but send him a text. Just a short but sweet one: **Hi, I'm the lady from the train, how are you?**

He replied and we exchanged quite a few more texts. The conversation seemed to flow easily and, at first, it focused on general getting to know each other: *Where do you live? Where do you work?* That sort of thing.

Eventually the messages moved on slightly: *What are you looking for in a man? Are you looking for something serious or not?*

About a week later, after some really flirty messages, we started to talk on the phone too. His voice was lovely and he sounded husky but with a gentle nature.

Our phone chats were something I quickly started to look forward to. We had so many things in common; we had similar childhoods, no siblings but loving parents, and we both currently worked in the city. One very important point was that neither of us had any children. One topic led to another, and we seemed to never run out of things to say.

Soon the chats led us on to conversations about our favourite places to go and to eat. We agreed on somewhere we'd both previously been to eat at, but on separate occasions, of course; I'd know if I had laid my eyes on him before.

After we'd made plans for our first date, I sat down to digest it all. I'd hit the jackpot here, so I thought I'd have a look at my list and see what I could tick.

Number 6:   *Has loads of money (a good job will do).* Well, part of it I knew to be true, but I was sure he was rich by the way he dressed.

Number 7:   *Nice teeth.* I'd seen them and they were perfect.

Number 10:   *NO CHILDREN.* I couldn't imagine why anyone would lie that they didn't have children, so I could safely say he had no children.

The night we'd agreed to meet came around, and I was very nervous; I really didn't want anything to mess this up. I decided to wear something that said sophisticated and classy; after all, I needed to make a good impression. My makeup and hair I chose to do subtly, though: not too much at once. I was going to bag this man and live in a very beautifully built house, one that left visitors' mouths open.

We were meeting at a very nice Italian restaurant; whilst having one of our very friendly phone chats we'd realised we didn't live that far apart either.

I had my usual two gin and tonics while getting ready and I was off. I felt a little more nervous than I had for the others, and maybe it was because this time I'd finally found Mr Right.

As I walked into the restaurant, I saw him waiting at our table for me; he was dressed immaculately in a bright white shirt and smart dark jeans that showed off his tan even more. He actually looked like a very wealthy man and reminded me a bit of George Clooney. I noticed he looked impressed with me too and smiled very nicely at me as I approached the table, showing his amazingly white straight teeth. *I need his babies,* I was thinking.

All evening we chatted about anything and everything, and

it all still flowed wonderfully. He told me about all his amazing work trips abroad and buildings he had designed. I smiled and laughed, constantly thinking, *Oh, yes, I could get used to that life.*

The night drew to an end, and I really didn't want it to, because by now I was totally smitten. He gave the waiter a nod to bring the bill and, although I offered to pay towards it, he insisted on paying it himself: a true gentleman.

Outside the air must have hit us both after we'd emptied the contents of four bottles throughout the evening. That was when he leant in for a kiss.

I didn't want him to think I was easy, but I also wanted to snog his face off. I felt my motto coming on. I just naturally couldn't help myself, so I reciprocated.

It was going fantastically for a minute or two, but then I realised I could feel something in my mouth, and it wasn't his tongue any more.

Er. Er, his teeth were in my mouth.

I reacted almost instantly and spat them out onto the pavement. To my shock, he picked them up and put them back in his mouth. He then told me I was out of order for doing that.

Everything was going in slow motion and I was thinking, *Is this guy serious? Your false teeth have just come out in my mouth.*

All my dreams of me and him were gone in that split second, and I couldn't believe he was telling me off for spitting them onto the ground. Because of the sheer shock I was in, I just told him I was sorry and walked away.

As I walked up the road, I started saying to myself, *Why am I apologising? Why am I so polite?* What I really should have said was 'Glue your false teeth in properly next time, loser!'

Oh, well, at least he paid the bill.

Dear God, I thought, *do not put him on my train on Monday morning.* I hoped he would never be on my commute to work again, for that matter.

1. Good sense of humour
2. ~~Tall (with big feet)~~
3. ~~Speaks Latin (Italian or Spanish will do)~~
4. Has loads of money (a good job will do)
5. ~~Nice teeth~~
6. ~~Nice home~~
7. ~~Good-looking~~
8. Good listener
9. ~~Good kisser~~
10. NO CHILDREN (well, not until they're with me)

CHAPTER 8
Blind Date

My good friend Sally, who I use to work with every day, had got a promotion and had been moved upstairs to the boss's level. I, however, had been kept in the same position for the last ten dedicated years I'd worked here, and now I realised I had to stay on this floor with the younger and less experienced staff alone.

I'd seen Ian a couple of times and, although he'd attempted to talk to me, I'd just politely made myself look busy. The truth was that I didn't know what to say about his secret of crossdressing and I really had to hold in my laughing fits around him, as I didn't want to upset him or bring any attention to the fact I'd been on a date with him.

I missed Sally, though, and more than ever I had to sit listening to the younger girls laughing and joking about how wonderful their lives were.

When Sally and I had the chance, we took a coffee break around the same time so we could have a catch-up and laugh about Suzie. I'd confided in her the day after our date. She was just as shocked as I was.

Today, on our coffee break together, she told me about her boyfriend's friend who apparently might be worth going on a date with. 'If nothing else,' she said, 'at least he has a really good job.' He had also recently broken up with his girlfriend and was back on the dating scene. My thought was that at least he'd be ticking number 4 on my list.

OK, Sally, I'll give it a go. Fix me up.

A few days later I got a call from her telling me he was really up for meeting me too. She gave me a place and time to meet him on the coming Saturday. This was very soon, but it was also very exciting. Maybe it would be just what I needed after all my previous dates going so terribly wrong. Maybe this was my Mr Right.

Saturday morning, I woke up feeling really positive about my date in the evening. We would be meeting at a nice wine bar in the city, which sounded good to me.

I did all my usual Saturday routines that morning: getting stocked up with food and wine, doing all my laundry and cleaning my flat.

That evening I played my favourite song, No Doubt, 'Don't Speak', which I always played when I was trying to get Ralph out of my head. I started getting ready and made sure I was wearing something eye-catching again. I had a few more drinks than I usually did when getting ready, but I felt great. I ordered my taxi and, while I was waiting, I changed my shoes a few times, then decided to go with the black strappy heels.

As the taxi approached the bar I quickly reapplied my lippy, then jumped out.

As I walked through the door, I saw someone of the description Sally gave me. *Oh, shit, no,* I thought. *Please, please, please don't let that untidy-looking man in the football T-shirt be him. He hasn't even brushed his hair.*

First thought: he's made no effort, so no way. I walk in looking like a movie star compared to him, and he's sitting there looking almost homeless. I wouldn't have minded so much if he'd at least been wearing one of the big football teams' shirts, but oh no, he was wearing a pissing Derby County shirt. When you're meeting someone from Nottingham, that's definitely not going to go down well.

My second thought: what a loser, in more ways than one.

Although I really didn't want to, I walked over to the table and introduced myself. 'Hi, I'm Chrissy.'

He looked at me, puzzled. Maybe I was at the wrong table, thank God.

'Hi, I'm Tom,' he replied.

Shit, I thought, *no, it's the right table, but definitely not Mr Right, looking like that.*

Still, I sat down. I'd give this a go; what else did I have to lose? I was desperately seeking, remember. I'd need to find a sperm donor if all else failed, so I might as well at least try to get on with the Derby County fan.

Throughout the evening talk was small and never really took root. We clearly didn't have anything in common, and I was definitely regretting the tight black dress. He constantly made comments about it. 'That's a nice dress.' 'How did you get in there?' He even asked how long it took me to get on and if I could get out of it just as quickly. Very inappropriate, to say the least, but you could say this was your average perverted football fanatic loser.

Although I wasn't keen on his comments about my outfit, it at least directed him away from the topic of football. *Boring*, I kept thinking. Did this bloke even know where his team sat in the league? I could bloody tell him right now: nowhere. Were they even in any league? I was sure I remembered my dad telling me they'd been relegated again.

His boring waste-of-time chatter eventually stopped, and the barman rang for last orders. I had already drunk so much, but, being my overly polite self, still nodded and smiled to accept one last drink for the road.

We eventually ended up outside, hoping to flag a taxi. That was when he asked me, 'Shall I come back to yours?'

I pondered this as I swayed, totally intoxicated. I clearly wasn't in any position to be turning anyone down, and my dating track record was proof of that, so like an idiot I agreed.

Back at mine I went to fix us both a drink in the kitchen, but when I returned to the living room I smelt something really disgusting, and it definitely wasn't me or my flat. I had no pets either.

I soon realised he'd taken off his shoes and had completely stunk out the place. My home now smelt like a flat that had ten cats and a neglected litter tray.

This is one very big stinking mistake, I thought to myself. How could I get out of this now?

I excuse myself to use the bathroom. The truth was that I really couldn't breathe out there any more, so I sat on the toilet for a while, thinking about what I could say to make him leave.

I know: I'll pretend I'm getting a very serious call, some sort of family emergency, and say I'll have to head out immediately. Yes, that should work.

As I returned to the living room, I took a deep breath. I awkwardly picked my phone up off the side table and played the ringtone. He didn't even notice as he was nearly falling asleep. I then pretended to take a serious emergency call and played the part of a very worried family member.

'I'm very sorry, but I'm going to have to go out,' I said to him.

To my surprise and horror this very drunk and very stinky man sat there and said, 'It's OK; you go, and I'll wait till you get back.'

Think, Chrissy, think!

Thinking quickly on my feet, I said, 'Oh, no, from the sound of it I won't be back in any hurry, so you'll have to leave. I'll call you a cab.'

He seemed to digest this and accepted by nodding. Phew!

Twenty long minutes later the taxi arrived, and he got in it.

'I'll call you,' he shouted out the window to me, but as it pulled away I uttered under my breath, 'Don't bother.' Another shit date to add to my list. I was going to kill Sally in the office on Monday.

I sit alone in my empty and now smelly flat, wondering what I was going to do now. I'm not a quitter, but I was so tired and seemed to be losing my faith in finding a good man altogether.

I got my list out and immediately crossed off number 4. Has a good job but completely stinks: no, thanks.

1. *Good sense of humour*
2. ~~*Tall (with big feet)*~~
3. ~~*Speaks Latin (Italian or Spanish will do)*~~
4. ~~*Has loads of money (a good job will do)*~~
5. ~~*Nice teeth*~~
6. ~~*Nice home*~~
7. ~~*Good-looking*~~
8. *Good listener*
9. ~~*Good kisser*~~
10. *NO CHILDREN (well, not until they're with me)*

CHAPTER 9
Old School Friend Date

After airing out my flat and trying to clear out my head too, I sat on one of my lonely nights, drinking too much and stalking Ralph and co. I was really sick of seeing his profile picture changing so regularly to a new and slightly different photograph of him drooling all over her juicy watermelons. I just couldn't stop looking, though. My life had been totally ruined, whilst he was there with the three of them, having fun.

I decided to draw myself away from their pictures for a minute and noticed I had a new message in my inbox. That was when I realised I'd been privately messaged by Stuart, an old school friend who I could vaguely remember.

I immediately started to look through his pictures. Mmm, he was looking very good in his late thirties, and much better than I remembered him at school; I seemed to remember him as being scruffy and very short. He certainly had improved and grown with age. There also didn't seem to be any pictures of children, or a wife, for that matter. There were pictures of a couple of women, but nothing cosy-looking; they looked more like friends on a night out.

Although I felt totally fed up with men, I sat and had a think about it. Maybe I should message him back and see how he was too; after all, we were old school friends. So, after another glass of wine, I started to type.

> **Hi Stuart, I'm fine thank you and doing really well,** I lied. **How are you?**

Two days later I got a message back. Obviously I was glad I'd had time to sober up, but I wondered what had taken him two days. Could it just be he didn't stalk people like me, or was he really that busy?

Anyway, I was glad to hear from him and, after feeling totally deflated by all these very strange dating experiences I had been having, it might be nice just to catch up with an old friend with no strings attached, if that was even possible. I messaged back straight away.

Throughout that day we exchanged quite a few messages. He asked me outright if I had any children. I said no. He made it very clear that this was great, and he definitely did not have any children either. Number 10 on my list ticked straight away, but I guess you could say it was half a tick, as it seemed he didn't want any in the future. Never mind, I thought, as he was just a friend.

We continued to send each other messages online. Eventually we exchanged telephone numbers and I said I'd call him the next day.

He was such an attentive listener and didn't seem to mind the fact that I'd rant on about my useless ex-boyfriend. Stuart soon became my agony aunt. He was better at listening than my good friend Sally, and he didn't butt in and start ranting on about his own relationship problems.

All day at work I kept thinking about him; could this be my chance at happiness? Then I'd think, *No, this is just an old school friend, nothing more.*

Later that day, when I called him, we reminisced on our school days, and it seemed he had a much better recollection of it all than me. He had me in stitches with stories of memories I'd buried away.

He even said that once we had shared a kiss. This I totally couldn't remember. Had I forgotten because he was a rubbish kisser, or was he lying that we'd already done it, so we might as well do it again?

Either way, he was an old friend and that was it. This was not happening. Well, not that quickly, anyway, and not after kissing Nice Teeth Guy on the first date; look where that got me. Yuck.

*

After many late-night phone calls, Stuart was really growing on me, and when he eventually asked me to go for something to eat with him – just as friends, of course – I jumped at the chance. He made me laugh and took my mind off Ralph and the misery he'd put me through. We agreed on a nice Chinese restaurant in town; it was one of my favourites.

It was all arranged for that weekend, so I only had a couple of days to prepare. I wanted to make a real effort this time, so I decided to buy something new. I knew if I ordered something online it wouldn't be delivered on time, and if it didn't fit properly, which happens 99% of the time, I would have no time to exchange it, so I decided I'd head straight for town after work the next day.

On my coffee break with Sally, I asked her if she wanted to come and help me choose something for my special date. Sally said she would, but I think it was only her way of making it up to me after fixing me up with Stig of the Dump.

I already had an outfit in mind: a figure-hugging trouser suit with heels. I imagined having my hair up in a tidy bun, and then at some point in the night I could mesmerise Stuart by undoing my bun to reveal my long dark locks. You know, like the girl in the shampoo advert. I bet she would never get dumped by her boyfriend.

The next day Sally and I headed for town and straight for the high street. We looked in a couple of shops, but nothing caught my eye, then we went into a lovely boutique that sold one-off outfits. I loved these little boutiques as there would be no chance of sharing an outfit with someone who looked far better in it than me.

I found what I needed; it was a tight jumpsuit rather than a trouser suit, but it had the perfect jacket to wear with it. I was going to look very sophisticated and very sexy.

This could be my chance to be happy, and so what if it seemed Stuart didn't want any children in the way? I guess I could understand that too, especially when you're on your annual leave and you just want to fly somewhere nice and hot to sunbathe all day, drinking piña coladas. The last thing you need is the kids ruining it.

On the night of our date, I was very nervous but excited to see him after all these years. I just hoped he really did look like the pictures on his social media page. I must say I was looking fine, and my new suit really complimented my curvy figure. As I had planned, I wore my hair up, but I decided to go for a ponytail to make me look more youthful.

I was on time to the restaurant, but he hadn't arrived yet, so I ordered myself a quick tipple, as you do, and sat and waited.

After what seemed like eternity, with people staring at me and wondering whether I had been stood up, I began to ask myself the same question, so I discreetly took out my phone to send him a text. Just then I heard someone call out my name.

I looked up to see the most handsome, strong-looking man. I nearly fainted, but I kept my consciousness and looked around at the people who had been watching me, giving them a very smug smile. Wow, my luck was definitely changing, and I knew at that moment that we were going to be more than just old school friends.

I had to compose myself, though, because I certainly didn't want him thinking I was smitten. Taking a deep breath, I said to myself, *Play it cool, Chrissy, and you could be spending the rest of your life cuddled up to him. Who cares about any kids now?*

After our meal he suggested we go on to somewhere nice where we could have more drinks. *Yes, that sounds more like it,* I thought. Nice restaurants are great, but trendy wine bars for more drink sounded like just the treat I needed. This was living the life. (OK, well, only for tonight.)

We carried on walking through the town and came to a bar that was playing quite loud music. We both looked at each other and laughed. We must have read each other's minds; we were both thinking we were just a bit too old for somewhere like this, but then we laughed again and nodded in unison because we were also thinking, *What the fuck, let's do it.*

We went inside and headed for the bar. On our way I noticed everyone staring at us, probably thinking, *What are those two doing in here?* They seriously looked half our age. *Oh, just ignore them,* I said to myself.

As we got to the bar Stuart ordered us two large cocktails. Before we knew it, we had drunk cocktail after cocktail and were both slurring our words. By this point there wasn't really any point in talking any more, and then suddenly he grabbed my hand and pulled me onto the dance floor with him.

Until that point everything was going really well, but then, all of a sudden, he began dancing really weirdly. I know everyone has their own moves and I certainly wasn't the greatest of dancers myself, but he began thrusting as though his life depended on It. He literally looked like he was bonking an imaginary person and, although I'd drunk loads, I still knew this was not a very good look. I was, however, very pleased I wasn't on the receiving end of those thrusts, or I most certainly would be waking up with whiplash.

The track changed to 'Murder on the Dancefloor', and I nearly fell to the floor. *How appropriate,* I thought in that very

55

inappropriate moment. I loved this song and usually would have enjoyed dancing to it, but gradually I started moving away from him, and eventually I just had to get off the floor and went to sit back on a vacant stool at the bar.

Although he knew I was no longer dancing with him, he continued to do this awful dance, giving me these looks as though he thought he was doing great. This was not going to end well.

Could I really marry this man who seemed to be impersonating Mr Bean on ecstasy? No, he definitely wasn't for me and he definitely wasn't Mr Right.

After at least another unbearable ten minutes or so I waved him over. I tried to be as nice as I could, but said I had to leave because I'd totally forgotten I had to be up early in the morning. He seemed fine with this and left with me to put me into a cab.

As I was driven home, I couldn't help but feel totally gutted. I really liked him, but I couldn't imagine spending my life with someone I couldn't take to any family dos just in case he got on the dance floor and embarrassed us both. How much more could I take? I had to accept I was going to spend my life alone.

When I got back home, I quickly grabbed my list and crossed off number 8. I'd rather have someone who didn't listen to me at all than someone who did but danced like that. Embarrassing, to say the least.

I was indecisive about crossing number 10 off, though. I really did want children one day, hopefully soon, but I really couldn't see it happening now.

1. *Good sense of humour*
2. ~~*Tall (with big feet)*~~
3. ~~*Speaks Latin (Italian or Spanish will do)*~~
4. ~~*Has loads of money (a good job will do)*~~

5. ~~Nice teeth~~
6. ~~Nice home~~
7. ~~Good-looking~~
8. ~~Good listener~~
9. ~~Good kisser~~
10. NO CHILDREN (well, not until they're with me)

CHAPTER 10

My Ex-Boyfriend

I had come to the realisation that I was not going to find anyone to love me, and definitely not Mr Right. I sat thinking about my loser ex, missing him like mad. I really needed some help here. Although I'm not religious, I had prayed many times he would come back to me. I wasn't superstitious either, but I decided to ask the angels for a sign.

Just as I said it out loud my mobile phone pinged. I had received a message.

Hi babe, I'm really missing you and would love to see you. Please!!!

My heart started beating really fast; I couldn't believe it. Maybe he was the one after all. I mean, he never actually meant to hurt me.

What am I saying? He dumped me. But getting this text just as I asked the angels had to mean something, right?

We exchanged some texts in which he said he was no longer seeing Jessie with the big boobs and that she meant nothing to him. He said it wasn't the same as what we shared, but she just kept throwing herself at him. He had really missed me and regretted ever leaving me.

Why, oh, why are you meeting this jerk? All day I had this weird conversation with myself, talking myself into meeting him and then out of it again.

I was going to meet him, wasn't I? I'd been feeling low about all these rubbish dates I'd been having, and he'd texted me exactly as I'd asked for a sign. That had to mean something. What other choice did I have?

He said he'd left his big booby bimbo when he'd realised she wasn't me. I knew that was bullshit, but, again, what choice did I have? I'd go and meet him. Maybe he had changed, and we could have children and live happily ever after.

I had arranged to meet him at one of our old spots: a lovely wine bar. At least if all else failed I could get totally drunk and hang out with some of the guys I knew from the gay scene. Singing and dancing to Kylie Minogue's 'Spinning Around' was not my idea of a great night out (not any more, anyway), but maybe it wouldn't come to that. Maybe I'd be cuddled up in his arms by the end of the night if I liked what he had to say.

My stomach was turning as I walked through the door and saw him sitting there, waiting for me. I knew I was looking good in this light blue knee-length dress and strappy heels.

As soon as I sat down, he started grovelling. I actually couldn't believe he was grovelling now, but what had changed?

Then he said, 'The real reason I wanted to see you in person is because I wanted to ask you something.'

Here we go, I thought. *He's going to ask if he can use my parents' holiday home or ask for some of his rubbish things back. Oh, shit, yes, I remember now: I put them in the bin whilst drinking and crying into his T-shirt.*

Now he was talking about all the old plans we used to have. 'We can always try for a baby in a year or two.'

Was this the same man? How could I trust him, never mind have a baby with him? The old Ralph would never have said this. He sounded desperate if anything.

Over dinner we chatted and seemed to be having a really nice time. We still shared all the same interests, and I started to imagine the two of us being happy again like old times: taking walks in the park, playing our favourite love songs and doing all the lovely things that we used to, just like a normal couple again.

Just then I got a ping on my phone; it was my best friend Jayne. Her message asked me to call her urgently, so I excused myself from the table and went to the little girls' room. I was slightly worried, as Jayne had never sent me this kind of message.

After two rings Jayne answered. 'You're not going to believe this, but I've just seen something online that shocked me and made me burst out laughing at the same time.'

'What is it?' I asked.

'Well, you know that weird bloke you went on a date with?'

'Which one?' I asked, as they'd all been very strange.

'The one who wears women's clothes and works at your office.'

'Oh, yes, Ian,' I replied.

Jayne was laughing as she spoke. 'He's in a relationship now.'

'Oh, good for him, but what's this got to do with me? I'm in the middle of a date here, Jayne, with Ralph.'

Jayne started laughing even harder. Through the laughter she said, 'Chrissy, he's in a relationship with Ralph's big booby bimbo. His profile picture is of them together, and on his status he's in a relationship.'

'*What?* Are you sure?'

'Yes,' she replied.

So I quickly had a look at Ian's social media page too and, sure enough, there they were together. I wouldn't have minded so much, but he was dressed as Suzie. He'd come out! Well, good for the two of them, if that was what they both wanted. This only meant one thing.

Right now, I was furious. So all this bullshit from Ralph about how much he'd missed me was really a rebound after being dumped for Suzie. I might be desperate, but I wasn't that desperate. If there was one thing I'd learnt through this whole experience, it was that I was going to be alright on my own.

I finished the call and thanked Jayne for the heads-up. I returned to the table and politely said to Ralph, 'Babe, I'm sorry, but I'm thinking things between us aren't going to work out, and you really deserve someone much better than me. Hope you find what you want in life.' With that I got up and walked out and felt absolutely fantastic.

When I got home I crossed number 10 off my list as it seemed finding someone with no kids was not a priority anymore, especially if they turned out to be like Ralph. Given the chance, I might be a great stepmother if I met someone with kids.

1. *Good sense of humour*
2. ~~*Tall (with big feet)*~~
3. ~~*Speaks Latin (Italian or Spanish will do)*~~
4. ~~*Has loads of money (a good job will do)*~~
5. ~~*Nice teeth*~~
6. ~~*Nice home*~~
7. ~~*Good looking*~~
8. ~~*Good listener*~~
9. ~~*Good kisser*~~
10. ~~*NO CHILDREN (well, not until they're with me)*~~

CHAPTER 11
Speed Dating

*I*t had been two weeks since that exhilarating night. I was in a different frame of mind after finding out that Ralph had been dumped by Jessie for Suzie; it was like a part of me felt satisfied that the universe had done its bit. The universe really did work in mysterious ways, I thought. He had been taught a lesson, and it had nothing to do with me. I felt guilt-free and satisfied; I'd now been the one to reject him, and it felt good.

Over the last couple of weeks, I hadn't thought about men or mending a broken heart. I'd even tried to sober myself up, in a fashion.

That was when my old school friend Helen rang me, the one who had moved down to London to be a successful reporter. *Here we go,* I thought, *ringing me to rub her success in my face,* but, strangely enough, she didn't mention how well she was doing; she was ringing to see how I was and ask if I was free at the weekend. She had been invited by one of her other successful friends to the opening of the friend's speed dating venue.

I jumped at the chance, as I was now living my life carefree and was always up for a good laugh. As a bonus I could also find love, but this really wasn't my intention now. I still didn't want to grow old on my own, though, so I had to keep an open mind.

I invited Helen to mine to get ready before we hit the town so we could have a few drinks and a good catch-up. Really, I felt the need to offload about what had happened with Ralph, but I could also tell her about all my unfortunate dates. I didn't feel ashamed any more about Ralph dumping me; I had totally picked myself up.

I was also very excited about speed dating as it sounded like such a trendy thing to do. It certainly was not my idea of dating, but I seemed to have tried everything else these past few months, and this year had truly turned out to be the worst of my life, so what the hell? At the very least I could have a good laugh, and it did have its perks; I could scan and vet a few men in a very short space of time. It could certainly be a good night out and, provided we were speed dating via a reputable provider and had a positive attitude, what could really go wrong?

*

As Saturday came around, I found myself thinking about what to wear for our big night out. I tried on several outfits before Helen turned up.

I settled on a red dress. Nothing like Suzie's red dress, of course; I definitely didn't have her legs. I also decided I'd wear my hair pulled back, so it stretched out a few of my wrinkles and took a few years off me.

When Helen arrived, we had a really long hug and I realised how much I had missed her and her friendship. We threw back some drinks and had a good laugh about some of my messed-up dates. She did say 'I told you so' about Ralph, but at this point I didn't care any more and didn't take it too much to heart. If anything, I agreed with her that I was worth ten of him.

Soon we ordered our taxi and headed down to her friend's event.

As we walked in, I quickly scanned the other people in the room. None of them took my fancy, but I said to myself that tonight was really about trying something new and having a bloody good laugh.

I took the seat that I was shown to, and then when we were

all seated this lady started to read out the rules. She told us she would ring a bell to tell us when it was time to switch. 'You'll get four minutes with each person, then the girls will move on to the next person to their left, with a pause of two minutes in between to make notes. The brief time period means you're not stuck with anyone you don't hit it off with, but have enough time to identify those you do.'

My heart was pounding, and my hands felt shaky, so I put them on my lap. The man opposite me looked way too old to be dating, and especially speed dating; how the heck would he keep up? Still, being the man, at least he didn't have to switch seats.

Our four minutes had started and, after we'd introduced ourselves, he asked me what I thought of the royal family. I nearly spat my drink out with laughter. What? Was he being serious? I made small talk with him about the royals but could tell his obsession with the Queen was very unhealthy.

Then the lady rang the bell. I was relieved to be moving, but seeing who I was moving towards was shockingly scary. I had never seen anyone so hairy: long hair and beard, and even his eyebrows needed a trim. What the heck was going on? Where were all the gorgeous young (but not too young) eligible bachelors?

As I had no choice, I sat down and started listening to him going on about how people needed to be empowered by their energy and spirit. He had a point, I thought, but shouldn't he be saving this for some spiritual retreat somewhere hot?

As he was banging on, my thoughts wandered to whether he had food bits inside his long beard, and I started to look it over. I couldn't see any evidence, but the thought made me feel sick. All I wanted to do was get wasted and maybe cop off with a nice handsome bloke. My chances of that were looking slim, but I knew I had to remain positive.

Just then she rang the bell again for us to switch. I had a couple of minutes to make notes, but all I wrote down was *get me out of here* and *LOSERS* in capital letters, then I had a giggle to myself.

Moving left, I could see someone who really resembled Ralph. Oh, dear God, don't let it be him.

As I sat down, I realised it wasn't, but I couldn't focus properly on his attempts to make conversation because the resemblance was so distracting. Part of me wanted to mouth off at him, and another part of me wanted to laugh in his face. All I knew was that I couldn't really look at him without thinking of Ralph, so this was not the man for me.

Luckily for me, the lady rang the bell for us to change seats again.

I jumped up as soon as I could, only to be disappointed again when I sat down to face a rather strange-looking man who couldn't speak a word of English. Don't get me wrong, I had a B in Spanish and could speak some French too, but those clearly weren't the language he was speaking. I decided to sit down and just have a laugh whilst nodding as though I understood everything he said. My mum always said I had a way of making others feel better even when my own feelings were at stake. However, I wasn't sure whether I was making him feel better or uncomfortable with being laughed at.

Just then I was saved by the bell again. I moved over to the next seat as soon as I could, only to find myself facing a very small man who just kept laughing at me hysterically. My name wasn't that funny, but even that made him laugh. It honestly made me feel very self-conscious, and I wondered whether this was the universe's way of saying I shouldn't have sat laughing at my last date.

After a few more of these awkward but funny dates it was all over. Although I hadn't met any Mr Rights tonight, I had had a laugh and was really pleased to have tried it. Helen and I stayed after the dating had finished and carried on drinking and laughing about the whole experience.

The only expectation that was left on my list was number 1, and I knew that this was a sign that this was really what was important to me. I had an abundance of humour already, and whoever I might meet in the future would need it too. I had to keep this in mind and just be OK with it. No more looking for anyone to share my life with; I was going to accept that I was fine by myself. Tonight had shown me just how important my friends were, and I promised myself to make much more of an effort to be a good friend to Helen, Jayne and Sally.

1. *Good sense of humour*
2. ~~*Tall (with big feet)*~~
3. ~~*Speaks Latin (Italian or Spanish will do)*~~
4. ~~*Has loads of money (a good job will do)*~~
5. ~~*Nice teeth*~~
6. ~~*Nice home*~~
7. ~~*Good-looking*~~
8. ~~*Good listener*~~
9. ~~*Good kisser*~~
10. ~~*NO CHILDREN (well, not until they're with me)*~~

CHAPTER 12

How It All Ended

So, I'd figured by now that all this dating was not going well for me and I would rather not go on any more embarrassing dates. I decided I was just going to grow old alone and give this dating thing a knock on the head. I'd tried, and I had been through everything a girl could imagine over the past year. I was totally done now, and I had been left with no option but to live my life alone.

At least I'd be able to live my life without anyone asking me why I was drinking so much wine every night or not bothering to shave my legs. I'd also be without anyone expecting me to pick up their dirty boxers after them, or knickers in Suzie's case. Maybe spinster life wasn't such a bad idea after all.

One thought that was still bothering me was the fact that I would never have any children; well, children of my own. Still, though, every time I saw a woman shouting at her kids and pulling her hair out, looking old and drained, I'd feel comfort at the thought of looking youthful for my age and not having that kind of stress every day. I could book exotic holidays and go to the spa every weekend if I chose to – so long as I could afford these things, of course.

My thoughts swayed back and forth every day with the pros and cons of other methods for becoming a parent. Maybe I could look into fostering or adopting in the future, but I'd have to save a bit and stop living in my overdraft first; I'm sure I wouldn't be accepted with my kind of debt.

I had to admit, though, that sometimes, looking at the

prospect of spending my life alone, I was left empty and depressed.

Ralph would never have another chance with me because he had thrown away what we had for a bit of fun and, although I was desperate for someone to love me, I refused to be second best. Sure, I could have been dumped for much worse, but still, being dumped for anyone is soul-destroying and I needed to repair that hurt.

Over the past few weeks since seeing Ralph, I had tried to pick myself up and carry on as best I could. It certainly had got easier now that I knew he'd been dumped too. I was getting over him, and I had stopped stalking him, as his profile pictures weren't that good anyway. Just him with his old work friends who he used to despise. Clearly now he was the desperate one.

However desperate I was, or should I say *had been*, I had had too many failed dates to care about having another. Every other aspect of my life was going well (apart from finances), or at least well enough, but for some unknown reason I couldn't find love again. Was I cursed? Was I being punished for something I had done in a past life? I didn't know; all I knew was that I was alone, and that was how it was going to stay. I'd definitely given up on dating.

Well, with all said and done, the least I could do was make myself another list, this one of things not to go for in a man. I was going to get it laminated and put on my fridge, just to remind myself every day of the weird men I needed to avoid.

1. NO *foot fetishists*
2. NO *gay Spanish guys*
3. NO *shoplifters found online*
4. NO *crossdressing colleagues, no matter how well they kiss*

5. *NO gorgeous teenagers*
6. *NO stinky football fanatics*
7. *NO creeps on trains with false teeth*
8. *NO old school friends who can't dance*
9. *NO speed dating - well, maybe just for a laugh*

And, last but not least:

10. *NO EX-BOYFRIENDS (especially if they dumped you for another girl)*

I also decided, because my list-making skills were clearly one of my strongest points, I was going to make a list of all the things I would do in my new single life. I'd have this one laminated too, but maybe I'd have it beside my bathroom mirror so that every morning and night, while I was brushing my real teeth, I could read it to remind me of the most important things in life. Yes, that was what I would do.

1. *PUT ME FIRST*
2. *Make more time for my friends*
3. *Read self-help books*
4. *Meditate*
5. *Yoga*
6. *Listen to 'I am' affirmations daily*
7. *Cut down on red wine*
8. *Never go on any more waste-of-time dates*
9. *Think about other options for becoming a parent*

And, last but not least:

10. *Celebrate being single*

Just then the doorbell went, and I went to see who it was. Looking through the peephole, I could see there was a man standing there, holding a big bunch of flowers. He was probably at the wrong door.

When I opened the door, he handed me the flowers and said it was a delivery for a Chrissy. Ooh, how nice. Mum and Dad were the only ones who sent me flowers, so it must have been from them.

I opened the card, and to my surprise it read:

Hi, I know you don't know me, but I often see you in and around the area. I'm your neighbour from flat 4B and I wondered would you like to come on a date with me? Mike x

Oh, dear, could I really afford to say no? Here we go again!